Biarritz Travel Tips (France)

Discover the most up-to-date and amazing places to explore in Biarritz, along with current information and guides on when to go, what to do, and the best places to see.

Hudson Miles

Table Of Contents

Introduction

Chapters:

Introduction to Biarritz

Best Time to Visit

Getting There

Accommodation

Top Attractions

Outdoor Activities

Basque Culture and Cuisine

Shopping and Markets

Day Trips and Nearby Destinations

Practical Information

Events and Festivals

Transportation within Biarritz

Safety and Health

Sustainable Tourism

Language and Cultural Tips

Popular slang terms for everyday use in Biarritz

Conclusion

Introduction

Emily had always dreamed of visiting France, and finally, her opportunity arrived. She was excited but also nervous about navigating a foreign country on her own. That's when she discovered Biarritz Travel Tips, a comprehensive guide to exploring France's stunning Biarritz region.

Armed with the travel tips, Emily embarked on her adventure with confidence. The guide provided invaluable information about local customs, transportation options, and must-see attractions. It even included hidden gems and off-the-beaten-path recommendations.

Thanks to Biarritz Travel Tips, Emily effortlessly explored the beautiful beaches, indulged in delectable cuisine, and discovered charming villages. The guide's suggestions for local markets and restaurants allowed her to experience authentic French flavors.

Emily was grateful for the guide's advice on avoiding tourist traps and saving money, which allowed her to make the most of her budget. The tips on interacting with locals also helped her forge genuine connections and learn about the region's rich culture.

With Biarritz Travel Tips as her trusted companion, Emily's journey through France became a remarkable adventure filled with unforgettable moments. She returned home with a heart full of cherished memories and a newfound love for the enchanting Biarritz region, all thanks to the invaluable guidance provided by the travel guide.

Welcome to Biarritz Travel Tips, your ultimate guide to exploring the enchanting region of Biarritz in France. Whether you're a first-time visitor or a seasoned traveler, this comprehensive guide is designed to make your journey a memorable and successful one.

Biarritz, located on the southwestern coast of France, is a captivating destination known for its stunning beaches, rich history, and vibrant culture. From the breathtaking Atlantic coastline to the charming Basque architecture, this region offers a unique blend of natural beauty and cultural heritage.

Within the pages of this guide, you will find a wealth of information to help you navigate Biarritz with ease. Discover insider tips on the best time to visit, the most captivating attractions, and the hidden gems that only locals know about. Whether you're interested in surfing the world-class waves, indulging in mouthwatering Basque cuisine, or exploring historical landmarks, Biarritz Travel Tips has got you covered.

Immerse yourself in the local culture with our recommendations on festivals, markets, and traditional events. Learn about the Basque traditions and customs that make Biarritz a truly distinctive destination.

Additionally, this guide provides practical advice on transportation, accommodation options, and language tips to ensure smooth and hassle-free travel. You'll also find valuable insights on how to save money while maximizing your experience, as well as tips on interacting with locals to create meaningful connections.

Biarritz Travel Tips is your trusted companion, crafted by seasoned travelers who have explored the region extensively. Let this guide be your passport to an extraordinary adventure in Biarritz, where every moment is an opportunity to create cherished memories. Get ready to uncover the wonders of Biarritz and embark on a journey you will never forget.

Chapter 1

Introduction to Biarritz

Welcome to the stunning coastal city of Biarritz, nestled in the southwestern part of France. With its idyllic location on the Bay of Biscay and a rich blend of Basque and French culture, Biarritz is a captivating destination that offers a perfect mix of natural beauty, history, and leisure.

Biarritz holds a special place in history, initially gaining prominence in the 19th century as a fashionable getaway for European nobility. Today, it retains its charm and allure, attracting visitors from around the world with its picturesque beaches, majestic cliffs, and breathtaking sunsets.

As you wander through Biarritz's vibrant streets, you'll encounter an enchanting blend of architectural styles, ranging from elegant Belle Époque buildings to traditional Basque structures. This fusion reflects the unique cultural heritage of the region, where the Basque language, music, and sports intertwine with French influences.

Biarritz is renowned as a surfing paradise, drawing surfers of all levels to ride its legendary waves. The city's surfing culture permeates every corner, creating a laid-back and welcoming atmosphere that is hard to resist.

In addition to its natural wonders and outdoor activities, Biarritz offers a myriad of delights for food enthusiasts. Prepare to indulge in mouthwatering Basque cuisine, which combines fresh seafood, farm-fresh produce, and aromatic spices. Whether you're dining at a Michelin-starred restaurant or savoring pintxos (Basque tapas) at a local bar, the culinary experiences in Biarritz are sure to leave a lasting impression.

Biarritz is not just a place; it's an experience that stimulates the senses and captures the heart.

Chapter 2

Best Time to Visit

The best time to visit Biarritz largely depends on your personal preferences and the activities you wish to engage in. Here's a breakdown of the seasons in Biarritz to help you determine the ideal time for your visit:

Summer (June to August): Summer is the peak tourist season in Biarritz, thanks to its pleasant weather and vibrant atmosphere. The average temperature ranges from 20°C to 25°C (68°F to 77°F), making it perfect for enjoying the stunning beaches and partaking in water sports like surfing and swimming. However, be prepared for larger crowds and higher prices during this time.

Spring (March to May) and Autumn (September to November): These shoulder seasons offer milder temperatures, ranging from 15°C to 20°C (59°F to 68°F). The weather is generally pleasant, and you can enjoy quieter beaches and shorter lines at popular attractions. Springtime brings blooming flowers and lush green landscapes, while autumn showcases beautiful fall colors. It's a great time to explore the city, go hiking, and experience the local culture.

Winter (December to February): Biarritz experiences mild winters, with temperatures averaging around 10°C to 15°C (50°F to 59°F). While it may be too cold for swimming, winter can be an excellent time to visit if you prefer a more serene and peaceful atmosphere. You can enjoy winter walks along the coastline, cozy up in cafes, and take advantage of off-season rates for accommodations.

It's important to note that weather conditions can vary, so it's always a good idea to check the forecast before planning your visit. Additionally, if you're specifically interested in surfing, the best swells tend to occur during autumn and winter.

Overall, Biarritz has something to offer throughout the year, so choose a season that aligns with your preferences and desired activities, whether it's basking in the summer sun or embracing the tranquility of the shoulder seasons.

Chapter 3

Getting There

Getting to Biarritz is convenient and accessible, thanks to various transportation options. Here's a guide to help you navigate your way to this captivating coastal city:

By Plane: Biarritz-Anglet-Bayonne Airport (BIQ) is the nearest airport, located just 5 kilometers (3 miles) southeast of Biarritz city center. It offers domestic and international flights, making it easily accessible from major European cities. From the airport, you can take a taxi, use public transportation, or rent a car to reach your final destination in Biarritz.

By Train: Biarritz has a well-connected train station, offering regular services to and from major cities in France and neighboring countries. The high-speed TGV trains provide convenient connections to cities like Paris, Bordeaux, and Toulouse. The train station is centrally located, making it easy to access the city center and other parts of Biarritz.

By Car: If you prefer driving, Biarritz is accessible via well-maintained road networks. The A63 motorway connects Biarritz to other major cities in France and neighboring countries. The drive along the scenic coastline can be a delightful experience. However, do note that parking in Biarritz city center can be limited, especially during peak tourist seasons, so it's advisable to check parking options in advance or opt for accommodations that offer parking facilities.

By Bus: Biarritz is well-served by long-distance buses, providing connections to cities within France and other European destinations. The bus station is centrally located, making it convenient for travelers to access the city center and nearby attractions.

By Ferry: Biarritz does not have a direct ferry port. However, if you're traveling from the UK, you can take a ferry to nearby ports such as Bilbao or Santander in Spain, and then continue your journey to Biarritz by car or train.

Once you arrive in Biarritz, the city's efficient local transportation system, including buses and taxis, will help you navigate within the city and explore its various attractions.

Consider your preferences and travel plans to choose the most suitable mode of transportation to reach Biarritz, whether it's flying for convenience, taking the train for a scenic journey, or driving for flexibility.

Chapter 4

Accommodation

Biarritz offers a range of accommodation options to suit various budgets and preferences. Whether you're seeking luxury, boutique charm, or budget-friendly stays, you'll find something that fits your needs. Here are some popular types of accommodations in Biarritz:

Hotels: Biarritz boasts a selection of hotels, ranging from luxurious 5-star establishments to cozy boutique hotels. Many of these accommodations offer stunning ocean views, proximity to the beach, and convenient access to the city's attractions and amenities. From elegant resorts to charming family-run hotels, you'll find a diverse range of options to choose from.

Guesthouses and Bed & Breakfasts: For a more intimate and personalized experience, consider staying at a guesthouse or bed & breakfast. These accommodations often offer charming rooms, warm hospitality, and a homely atmosphere. They are a great choice if you prefer a more local and immersive experience.

Holiday Apartments and Vacation Rentals: If you're traveling with a group or prefer more space and privacy, renting a holiday apartment or vacation home can be an excellent option. Biarritz has a variety of self-catering accommodations available, ranging from stylish apartments to spacious villas. This choice allows you to have a home away from home and the flexibility to cook your meals.

Surf Camps and Hostels: Biarritz's popularity as a surfing destination has given rise to surf camps and hostels catering to surf enthusiasts and budget travelers. These accommodations provide a laid-back atmosphere, shared dormitories or private rooms, and often offer surf lessons and equipment rental. They are a great choice for solo travelers, backpackers, and those looking to meet fellow surfers.

Location-wise, you'll find accommodations in and around the city center, as well as options near the beach or in quieter residential areas. Consider your preferences, such as proximity to attractions, the beach, or public transportation when selecting your accommodation.

It's advisable to book your accommodation in advance, especially during peak tourist seasons, to secure the best rates and availability. Check online booking platforms or consult with a travel agent to find the perfect accommodation that suits your needs and enhances your stay in Biarritz.

Chapter 5

Top Attractions

Biarritz is a captivating coastal city that offers a plethora of attractions to explore. Here are some of the top attractions that you shouldn't miss during your visit:

Biarritz Beaches: Biarritz is renowned for its beautiful beaches that cater to different preferences. The Grand Plage is the main beach, with golden sands and vibrant atmosphere, perfect for sunbathing and people-watching. For surf enthusiasts, head to La Côte des Basques, a legendary surf spot with stunning views. Other notable beaches include Miramar Beach and Marbella Beach.

Rocher de la Vierge: This iconic rock formation sits in the middle of the Bay of Biscay and is accessed by a footbridge. Admire the panoramic views of the coastline and the crashing waves as you explore the rock and its surrounding area.

Musee de la Mer: Dive into the depths of the ocean at the Museum of the Sea. Discover fascinating marine life, including sharks, seals, and rays. The museum also houses exhibitions on whales, seahorses, and the history of Biarritz.

Phare de Biarritz: Located on a cliff overlooking the Bay of Biscay, the Biarritz Lighthouse offers breathtaking views of the coastline. Climb to the top for a panoramic vista of the ocean and the city.

Aquarium de Biarritz: Explore the wonders of the underwater world at the Biarritz Aquarium. Encounter a diverse range of marine species, including colorful fish, turtles, and jellyfish. Don't miss the fascinating shark tank and the interactive touch pools.

Le Musée Asiatica: Immerse yourself in Asian art and culture at this unique museum. The collection showcases a wide range of artifacts from countries such as India, Tibet, Nepal, and China, including sculptures, paintings, and textiles.

Les Halles de Biarritz: Indulge in a sensory feast at the lively covered market. Stroll through the stalls filled with fresh local produce, cheese, seafood, and Basque specialties. It's a great place to sample regional delicacies and soak up the vibrant atmosphere.

Sainte-Eugénie Church: Admire the beautiful architecture of this Neo-Gothic church, located in the city center. Step inside to appreciate its stunning stained glass windows and peaceful ambiance.

Golf de Biarritz Le Phare: If you're a golf enthusiast, visit the historic Biarritz Golf Course, one of the oldest in Europe. Enjoy a round of golf amidst picturesque surroundings and ocean views.

Basque Coast Geopark: Explore the rugged beauty of the Basque Coast Geopark, which stretches from Biarritz to Hendaye. Discover dramatic cliffs, hidden coves, and unique geological formations along the coastal trail.

These are just a few highlights among many attractions that Biarritz has to offer. Explore the city's charming streets, embrace its surf culture, and soak up the natural beauty that surrounds you. Biarritz promises a memorable and enriching experience for every visitor.

Chapter 6

Outdoor Activities

Biarritz, with its stunning coastal location and picturesque landscapes, offers a wealth of outdoor activities for nature lovers and adventure seekers. Here are some of the top outdoor activities you can enjoy in and around Biarritz:

Surfing: Biarritz is renowned as a premier surfing destination, attracting surfers from around the world. Whether you're a beginner or an experienced surfer, the city's beaches, such as La Côte des Basques and Grande Plage, offer excellent waves for all levels. Take a surf lesson, rent a board, and ride the waves in this surfing paradise.

Beach Activities: Apart from surfing, Biarritz's beaches provide plenty of opportunities for relaxation and recreation. Soak up the sun, take a refreshing swim, or simply enjoy a leisurely beach stroll along the sandy shores. You can also try beach volleyball, paddleboarding, or beach yoga.

Coastal Walks and Hikes: Discover the natural beauty of Biarritz by embarking on coastal walks and hikes. The scenic coastal trail offers breathtaking views of the rugged cliffs, pristine beaches, and the vast Atlantic Ocean. The Pointe Saint-Martin and Le Sentier du Littoral are popular routes that showcase the region's stunning landscapes.

Golfing: Biarritz is a golfer's paradise, with several world-class golf courses. Play a round of golf amidst stunning backdrops, such as the Biarritz Le Phare Golf Course or the Ilbarritz Golf Training Center. Enjoy the lush green fairways and the challenge of these scenic courses.

Cycling: Explore the city and its surroundings on two wheels. Biarritz offers bike rental services, allowing you to cycle along the coastline, visit nearby villages, or embark on longer rides through the scenic countryside. The Vélodyssée cycle route, which stretches along the Atlantic coast, passes through Biarritz and offers a fantastic cycling experience.

Hiking in the Pyrenees: Biarritz serves as a gateway to the Pyrenees Mountains. Take a day trip and go hiking in the Pyrenees, exploring picturesque trails and enjoying panoramic mountain views. Popular hiking destinations include the Rhune Mountain and the nearby Iraty Forest.

Watersports: In addition to surfing, Biarritz offers a range of other watersports to enjoy. Try your hand at paddleboarding, kayaking, or windsurfing in the calm waters of the Bay of Biscay. You can rent equipment and take lessons from local providers.

Horseback Riding: Discover the beauty of Biarritz's countryside on horseback. Several equestrian centers offer guided horseback riding excursions, allowing you to explore the scenic landscapes, ride along the beaches, or venture into the forests.

Paragliding: Experience the thrill of paragliding and soar above Biarritz's coastline, enjoying breathtaking aerial views of the city and the ocean. Tandem paragliding flights are available, allowing you to fly with an experienced pilot.

Whether you prefer a laid-back beach day, an adrenaline-filled adventure, or a peaceful hike, Biarritz offers an array of outdoor activities to cater to every interest and skill level. Embrace the natural beauty and active spirit of this coastal paradise.

Chapter 7

Basque Culture and Cuisine

Biarritz is located in the heart of Basque Country, and experiencing the vibrant Basque culture and cuisine is a must during your visit. Here's a glimpse into Basque culture and the delectable culinary delights you can savor in Biarritz:

Basque Culture:

Basque Language and Traditions: The Basque language, Euskara, is unique and unrelated to any other language in the world. You may encounter Basque street signs and hear locals conversing in this ancient language. Immerse yourself in Basque traditions, such as the Basque pelota (a traditional handball game) and Basque music, including the distinctive sounds of the txalaparta and trikitixa.

Basque Festivals: Basque people are known for their rich cultural festivals. If your visit coincides with one of these events, such as the Fête de Bayonne or the Biarritz Surf Festival, you'll have the opportunity to witness lively parades, traditional dances, and music performances.

Basque Architecture: Basque architecture is characterized by its unique style, blending traditional elements with influences from neighboring regions. Look out for traditional Basque houses known as "maisons laborieuses" with their half-timbered facades and vibrant red and green colors.

Basque Cuisine:

Pintxos: Basque cuisine is famous for its pintxos, small bite-sized snacks typically served on a slice of bread and held together with a toothpick. Biarritz boasts numerous pintxos bars where you can indulge in a variety of flavors and combinations, from traditional Basque ingredients like jamón, local cheeses, and fresh seafood.

Seafood Delights: Biarritz's coastal location means you can savor an abundance of fresh seafood. Treat yourself to succulent oysters, grilled sardines, Basque-style squid, and other delicious seafood dishes.

Axoa: This traditional Basque dish consists of minced veal or veal and pork cooked with onions, peppers, and Espelette pepper. It's a comforting and flavorful dish that showcases the region's culinary heritage.

Basque Cider: Basque Country is known for its cider production. Visit a local cider house, called a "sagardotegi," to sample the crisp and tart Basque cider straight from the barrel. It's often enjoyed alongside a hearty Basque meal.

Gateau Basque: Conclude your culinary journey with a slice of Gateau Basque, a traditional Basque cake filled with either custard or cherry jam. This buttery and indulgent dessert is a sweet treat to savor.

Don't forget to pair your culinary delights with a glass of Basque wine, such as the Txakoli or the red wines of Irouléguy, produced in the nearby vineyards.

Exploring Basque culture and indulging in Basque cuisine is an enriching experience that will provide a deeper understanding of the region's traditions and flavors. Take the opportunity to immerse yourself in the vibrant Basque way of life during your time in Biarritz.

Chapter 8

Shopping and Markets

Biarritz offers a delightful shopping experience, with a mix of trendy boutiques, local markets, and specialty stores. Whether you're looking for fashionable clothing, artisanal products, or local delicacies, here are some shopping destinations in Biarritz:

Les Halles de Biarritz: Located in the city center, Les Halles is a vibrant covered market where locals and visitors gather to shop for fresh produce, gourmet products, and regional specialties. Explore the stalls filled with colorful fruits, vegetables, cheese, seafood, charcuterie, and more. It's an ideal place to purchase local ingredients for a picnic or to indulge in Basque gastronomy.

Rue Mazagran: This lively street in Biarritz is lined with an array of fashionable boutiques, designer shops, and stylish concept stores. Discover unique clothing, accessories, and homeware from local and international brands. It's the perfect place for fashion enthusiasts to find trendy pieces or shop for souvenirs.

Rue Gambetta: Located in the city center, Rue Gambetta offers a mix of boutiques, specialty stores, and art galleries. Explore the charming streets and find unique items, including fashion, jewelry, home decor, and artwork. The pedestrian-friendly area allows for leisurely shopping and browsing.

Les Docks de la Négresse: This shopping complex, located on the outskirts of Biarritz, offers a range of retail outlets, including clothing stores, sportswear shops, furniture stores, and more. It's a convenient destination for those looking for a larger selection of brands and products.

Biarritz Market: Held every Saturday morning at Place Sainte-Eugénie, Biarritz Market is a lively open-air market where you can find a variety of goods, including fresh produce, regional products, clothing, accessories, crafts, and flowers. It's a great place to experience the local atmosphere and pick up unique souvenirs.

Antiques and Brocantes: Biarritz is home to several antique shops and brocantes (secondhand stores) where you can discover vintage furniture, collectibles, artwork, and curiosities. Rue Gardères is known for its concentration of antique shops, making it a treasure trove for antique lovers.

Basque Specialty Shops: Explore specialty shops in Biarritz that focus on Basque products and souvenirs. These stores offer a wide range of items, including Basque textiles, espadrilles, Basque berets, traditional Basque pottery, local jams and preserves, Basque knives, and more. They are perfect for finding authentic Basque mementos and gifts.

When shopping in Biarritz, keep in mind that most stores and markets are closed on Sundays, and some may have limited hours during lunchtime. Take your time to browse, interact with friendly shopkeepers, and immerse yourself in the shopping culture of Biarritz.

Chapter 9

Day Trips and Nearby Destinations

Biarritz is a perfect base for exploring the picturesque region of Basque Country and beyond. Here are some day trip options and nearby destinations that you can consider during your visit:

Bayonne: Just a short distance from Biarritz, the charming city of Bayonne is known for its rich history and cultural heritage. Explore the narrow streets of the old town, visit the stunning Bayonne Cathedral, and indulge in the city's famous chocolate and traditional Basque cuisine. Don't miss the opportunity to witness the colorful Bayonne Festival held in July.

Saint-Jean-de-Luz: Located along the Basque coast, Saint-Jean-de-Luz offers a mix of beautiful beaches, historical sites, and a vibrant town center. Visit the picturesque harbor, stroll along the pedestrian streets, and explore the Maison Louis XIV, where the famous Sun King got married. Enjoy fresh seafood at one of the waterfront restaurants and take in the relaxed ambiance of this coastal gem.

San Sebastián, Spain: Cross the border into Spain and visit the stunning city of San Sebastián, just 40 kilometers from Biarritz. Known for its world-class culinary scene, beautiful beaches, and iconic architecture, San Sebastián is a must-visit destination. Take a leisurely walk along La Concha Beach, sample pintxos (Basque tapas) in the atmospheric Old Town, and enjoy the vibrant atmosphere of this cultural hub.

Espelette: Nestled in the foothills of the Pyrenees, Espelette is a charming village known for its famous Espelette peppers. Stroll through the picturesque streets adorned with vibrant red pepper strings, visit the Pepper Museum, and explore the local shops offering a variety of pepper-based products. Don't forget to taste dishes spiced with this iconic ingredient.

The Pyrenees Mountains: Biarritz is a gateway to the Pyrenees Mountains, offering breathtaking landscapes and outdoor activities. Take a day trip to explore the mountain range, go hiking in the scenic valleys, visit charming villages like Ainhoa or Sare, or even take the scenic Petit Train de la Rhune to enjoy panoramic views from the summit.

Biarritz Hinterland: Venture into the picturesque countryside surrounding Biarritz, known as the "Biarritz Hinterland." Discover quaint villages such as Arcangues and Bidart, with their traditional Basque architecture and peaceful ambiance. Explore the rolling hills, vineyards, and enjoy the scenic beauty of the Basque countryside.

Dax and its Thermal Spas: Located to the northeast of Biarritz, Dax is renowned for its thermal spas and wellness treatments. Indulge in a rejuvenating spa experience, relax in the hot springs, and immerse yourself in the therapeutic benefits of the region's natural resources.

These are just a few examples of the many day trip options and nearby destinations you can explore from Biarritz. Whether you prefer historical cities, coastal towns, or mountain landscapes, the region surrounding Biarritz offers a diverse range of experiences to suit every interest.

Chapter 10

Practical Information

When traveling to Biarritz, it's helpful to have some practical information to ensure a smooth and enjoyable trip. Here are some practical tips and information to keep in mind:

Visa Requirements: Check the visa requirements for your country of residence before traveling to Biarritz, France. Ensure that your passport is valid for at least six months beyond your intended stay.

Currency: The currency in France is the Euro (€). It's advisable to carry some cash with you for small purchases and to have a credit card for larger transactions. ATMs are widely available in Biarritz, and credit cards are accepted at most establishments.

Language: The official language of France is French. While visiting Biarritz, you'll encounter locals who predominantly speak French.

However, many people in the tourism industry and popular areas may also speak English, especially in hotels, restaurants, and shops.

Weather: Biarritz has a temperate oceanic climate, characterized by mild winters and warm summers. The summer months (June to August) are the most popular for tourists, with average temperatures ranging from 20°C to 25°C (68°F to 77°F). However, the weather can be changeable, so it's a good idea to pack layers and be prepared for occasional rainfall.

Transportation: Biarritz is well-connected by various transportation options:

By Air: Biarritz Pays Basque Airport (BIQ) is located about 5 kilometers from the city center and serves domestic and international flights.

By Train: Biarritz has a train station with regular connections to major cities in France and neighboring countries. The train station is centrally located, making it convenient to explore Biarritz and its surroundings.

By Car: Biarritz is easily accessible by car, with well-maintained road networks. Rental car services are available at the airport and in the city.

Public Transportation: Biarritz has an efficient local bus network, making it easy to navigate the city and nearby areas. There are also taxis and rideshare services available for convenient transportation.

Safety: Biarritz is generally a safe destination for travelers. However, it's always advisable to take standard safety precautions, such as being aware of your surroundings, keeping your belongings secure, and avoiding isolated areas at night.

Time Zone: Biarritz operates on Central European Time (CET), which is UTC+1 during standard time. It observes Daylight Saving Time, so during daylight saving months, it follows Central European Summer Time (CEST), which is UTC+2.

Electrical Outlets: In France, the standard voltage is 230V, and the frequency is 50Hz. The plugs used are Type C and Type E. If your devices use a different type of plug or voltage, you may need a travel adapter or converter.

Wi-Fi and Internet: Most hotels, restaurants, and cafes in Biarritz offer free Wi-Fi access. Additionally, you can find internet cafes throughout the city if you need to access the internet or make international calls.

Emergency Numbers: In case of emergencies, the general emergency number in France is 112 for police, medical assistance, or fire services. Familiarize yourself with the local emergency numbers as well.

Remember to check the latest travel advisories and guidelines before your trip to ensure you have the most up-to-date information. With these practical tips, you can make the most of your visit to Biarritz and have a memorable experience.

Chapter 11

Events and Festivals

Biarritz is a vibrant city that hosts various events and festivals throughout the year, offering visitors a chance to immerse themselves in the local culture and festivities. Here are some notable events and festivals to look out for when planning your trip to Biarritz:

Biarritz Surf Festival: As a renowned surfing destination, Biarritz celebrates its surf culture with the annual Biarritz Surf Festival. This multi-day event features professional surfing competitions, exhibitions, film screenings, live music performances, and beachside activities. Surf enthusiasts from around the world gather to witness the thrilling waves and enjoy the lively atmosphere. The festival typically takes place in July.

Fête de Bayonne: Known as one of the largest festivals in France, the Fête de Bayonne is a festive celebration of Basque culture and traditions. Held in nearby Bayonne, this event spans over five days in July and attracts thousands of visitors. Expect lively street parades, traditional Basque music and dance performances, vibrant costumes, bullfighting events, fireworks, and an overall festive ambiance.

Biarritz Quiksilver Maïder Arosteguy: This annual surfing competition takes place in April and attracts amateur and professional surfers from all over Europe. It's a great opportunity to witness impressive surf skills and enjoy the exciting atmosphere on the beaches of Biarritz.

Les Fêtes Musicales de Biarritz: This classical music festival brings together talented musicians from France and around the world. Held in various venues across Biarritz, including churches and concert halls, the festival offers a diverse program of orchestral performances, chamber music recitals, and solo concerts. It usually takes place during the summer months.

Biarritz Beer Festival: For beer enthusiasts, the Biarritz Beer Festival is a must-attend event. This festival showcases a wide selection of craft beers from local and international breweries. Visitors can sample different beer styles, attend workshops and tastings, and enjoy live music performances. The festival typically takes place in September.

Basque Pelota Tournaments: Basque pelota is a traditional handball game popular in the Basque Country. Biarritz hosts regular tournaments where you can watch skilled players compete in this fast-paced and thrilling sport. Check the local schedule for upcoming matches and experience the excitement firsthand.

Christmas Market: During the festive season, Biarritz transforms into a winter wonderland with its Christmas Market. Stroll through the festively decorated stalls, sip on mulled wine, and browse a variety of artisanal products, handicrafts, and local delicacies. The market is a perfect place to find unique gifts and immerse yourself in the holiday spirit.

These are just a few of the many events and festivals that take place in Biarritz throughout the year. The city's lively calendar ensures there's always something exciting happening, offering visitors a chance to experience the local culture, traditions, and entertainment during their stay.

Chapter 12

Transportation within Biarritz

Getting around Biarritz is convenient and straightforward, thanks to its well-developed transportation system. Here are some transportation options for navigating the city:

Walking: Biarritz is a relatively small city, and many of its popular attractions, such as the beaches, city center, and shopping districts, are within walking distance of each other. Walking is an excellent way to explore the city, soak in its vibrant atmosphere, and discover hidden gems along the way.

Public Buses: Biarritz has an efficient local bus network operated by Chronoplus. The bus system covers the entire city, including popular tourist areas, and connects to neighboring towns. Bus tickets can be purchased directly from the driver or at designated ticket booths. It's advisable to check the bus schedules and plan your routes in advance.

Bicycle Rentals: Biarritz is a bike-friendly city with dedicated cycling lanes and paths. Renting a bicycle is a popular and eco-friendly way to get around. There are several bike rental shops in the city where you can hire bicycles for a few hours or even the entire day. Exploring Biarritz on two wheels allows you to enjoy the scenic coastal views and navigate the city at your own pace.

Taxis: Taxis are readily available in Biarritz and can be hailed on the street or found at designated taxi stands. You can also book a taxi in advance through local taxi companies or by using ride-hailing apps. Taxis are a convenient option for short trips or when you have heavy luggage.

Rental Cars: If you prefer the flexibility of having your own vehicle, rental cars are available at Biarritz Pays Basque Airport and in the city center. Having a car allows you to explore the surrounding areas and take day trips at your convenience. However, parking can be limited and expensive in some parts of the city, so it's important to check parking regulations and availability beforehand.

Electric Scooters: Electric scooters have become increasingly popular in Biarritz as a fun and efficient mode of transportation. Look out for electric scooter rental companies operating in the city. These scooters can be easily rented through smartphone apps, and you can enjoy the convenience of zipping around the city streets.

Biarritz's compact size and well-connected transportation options make it easy to navigate and explore the city and its surroundings. Consider the various modes of transportation based on your preferences, convenience, and the distances you plan to cover during your visit.

Chapter 13

Safety and Health

When it comes to safety and health in Biarritz, the city generally maintains a high standard of security and healthcare. However, it's always essential to prioritize your well-being during your travels. Here are some tips to ensure a safe and healthy stay in Biarritz:

General Safety: Biarritz is a relatively safe city, but it's advisable to take standard safety precautions. Keep an eye on your belongings, especially in crowded areas and tourist spots. Avoid displaying valuable items openly and be cautious of pickpockets. Stay aware of your surroundings, particularly at night, and stick to well-lit and populated areas.

Emergency Services: In case of emergencies, dial the European emergency number 112 for immediate assistance. This number connects you to police, medical services, or fire department, depending on the situation. Keep a note of important local emergency numbers as well.

Travel Insurance: It's recommended to have comprehensive travel insurance that covers medical emergencies, trip cancellations, and lost or stolen belongings. Ensure that your insurance policy includes coverage for any activities you plan to participate in, such as water sports or outdoor adventures.

Medical Facilities: Biarritz has a good healthcare system with medical facilities and hospitals that provide quality care. If you require medical assistance, there are several clinics, pharmacies, and hospitals available in the city. It's a good idea to carry any necessary prescription medications and familiarize yourself with the location of nearby medical facilities.

Sun Protection: Biarritz is a coastal city known for its beautiful beaches and sunny weather. Protect yourself from the sun by wearing sunscreen with a high SPF, a hat, sunglasses, and lightweight clothing. Stay hydrated, especially during hot summer months, and seek shade during peak sun hours.

Water Safety: Biarritz's beaches offer great opportunities for swimming and water activities. However, it's important to adhere to water safety guidelines. Observe warning flags and signs at the beaches, and swim only in designated areas with lifeguards present. Be cautious of strong currents and always supervise children when near the water.

Food and Hygiene: Biarritz boasts a diverse culinary scene, offering a variety of delicious dishes. Ensure you dine at reputable establishments and follow basic food and water hygiene practices. Drink bottled water if you have concerns about tap water quality, and wash your hands frequently, especially before eating.

By staying aware, taking necessary precautions, and looking after your health, you can enjoy a safe and enjoyable experience in Biarritz.

Chapter 14

Sustainable Tourism

Sustainable tourism is a growing focus worldwide, and Biarritz is no exception. The city recognizes the importance of preserving its natural and cultural heritage while promoting responsible and eco-friendly tourism practices. Here are some ways in which you can contribute to sustainable tourism in Biarritz:

Choose Eco-Friendly Accommodation: Look for hotels or accommodations that prioritize sustainability. Many hotels in Biarritz have implemented eco-friendly practices, such as energy-efficient systems, waste reduction, and water conservation measures. Consider staying at eco-certified accommodations or those that have implemented green initiatives.

Support Local and Sustainable Businesses: Patronize local businesses, such as restaurants, shops, and tour operators, that prioritize sustainable practices. Look for establishments that promote locally sourced products, organic options, and fair-trade goods. By supporting local businesses, you contribute to the local economy and help reduce the carbon footprint associated with long-distance transportation.

Reduce Plastic Usage: Plastic pollution is a global issue, and you can contribute to its reduction by minimizing your plastic usage. Carry a reusable water bottle and shopping bag to avoid single-use plastics. When dining out, choose restaurants that use sustainable packaging and offer plastic-free alternatives.

Respect the Environment: Biarritz is blessed with stunning natural landscapes, including its beaches, cliffs, and forests. Help preserve these environments by practicing responsible tourism. Follow designated paths and trails, avoid littering, and dispose of waste properly. Be mindful of local wildlife and refrain from disturbing or feeding them.

Use Sustainable Transportation: Opt for sustainable modes of transportation whenever possible. Walk or cycle around the city, taking advantage of Biarritz's pedestrian-friendly areas and dedicated cycling paths. Utilize public transportation, such as buses or trains, to reduce carbon emissions. If you need to rent a car, consider choosing a fuel-efficient or electric vehicle.

Conserve Water and Energy: Practice water and energy conservation in your accommodations. Limit your water usage by taking shorter showers and reusing towels when possible. Turn off lights, air conditioning, and other electronics when not in use to conserve energy.

Learn and Respect the Local Culture: Take the time to learn about the local culture, customs, and traditions of Biarritz and the Basque Country. Respect cultural sites, traditions, and local communities by adhering to guidelines and showing appreciation for their heritage.

Engage in Responsible Outdoor Activities: Biarritz offers numerous outdoor activities, such as surfing, hiking, and wildlife observation. Engage in these activities responsibly by following designated paths, respecting wildlife habitats, and supporting responsible tour operators who prioritize conservation and education.

By adopting sustainable tourism practices, you can help preserve the natural beauty of Biarritz for future generations to enjoy. Remember, even small actions can make a significant impact when it comes to sustainable tourism.

Chapter 15

Language and Cultural Tips

When visiting Biarritz, it's helpful to familiarize yourself with some language and cultural tips to enhance your experience and connect with the local community. Here are some suggestions:

Language: The official language of Biarritz, like the rest of France, is French. While many locals also speak English, it's appreciated when visitors make an effort to learn a few basic French phrases. Knowing greetings, simple pleasantries, and how to say "thank you" (merci) can go a long way in showing respect and fostering positive interactions.

Greetings: When meeting someone in Biarritz, it's customary to greet them with a handshake and a friendly "Bonjour" (Good day) or "Bonsoir" (Good evening) depending on the time of day. Addressing people with "Madame" (Mrs.) or "Monsieur" (Mr.) followed by their surname is also considered polite.

Punctuality: Punctuality is valued in French culture, so it's advisable to arrive on time for appointments, tours, or dinner reservations. Being punctual demonstrates respect for others' time and is considered good etiquette.

Dining Etiquette: When dining in Biarritz, it's common to wait for the host or the waiter to indicate where you should sit. Keep in mind that meals in France are often enjoyed slowly, with multiple courses. It's polite to wait until everyone is served before starting to eat and to keep your hands on the table during the meal.

Dress Code: Biarritz has a relaxed and casual atmosphere, but it's advisable to dress neatly when visiting restaurants, especially in the evening. While beachwear is appropriate for the beach, it's courteous to cover up when leaving the beach and entering public areas.

Tipping: Tipping in France is not obligatory, as a service charge is often included in the bill. However, leaving a small tip for exceptional service is appreciated. Typically, rounding up the bill or leaving a 5-10% tip is customary.

Respect for Cultural Sites: Biarritz has a rich cultural heritage, so it's important to show respect when visiting religious sites, monuments, or historical landmarks. Dress modestly and follow any guidelines or restrictions indicated at the site.

Be Polite: French culture values politeness, so remember to use "s'il vous plaît" (please) and "merci" (thank you) in your interactions. Politeness and courtesy go a long way in creating positive connections with locals.

Learn about Basque Culture: Biarritz is located in the Basque Country, where Basque culture has a significant influence. Take the opportunity to learn about Basque traditions, cuisine, and folklore. Respect and appreciate the unique cultural heritage of the region.

By embracing the local language and cultural customs, you can create a more immersive and enriching experience during your visit to

Biarritz. The locals will appreciate your efforts and it can lead to more meaningful connections and interactions with the community.

Popular slang terms for everyday use in Biarritz

Here is a list of popular slang terms for everyday use in Biarritz. Please note that slang terms can vary and evolve over time, so some of these may be more commonly used than others:

Allez: Let's go
Bouffer: To eat
Brek: Breakfast
Ciao: Goodbye
Ça va?: How are you?
Chaud: Hot
Chill: Relax
Cimer: Thanks
Dégage: Go away
Drôle: Funny
Fringues: Clothes
Génial: Awesome
Gosses: Kids
Graille: Food
J'suis crevé: I'm exhausted
Kiffer: To like/enjoy
La flemme: Can't be bothered

Les potes: Friends
Mec: Dude/guy
Meuf: Girl
Nul: Lame
Ouf: Crazy
Pécho: To flirt/hook up
Pote: Friend
Quoi de neuf?: What's up?
Raide: Very/totally
Rentrer: To go home
Rigoler: To laugh
Sérieux?: Seriously?
Tarpin: Very/extremely
Tchatcher: To chat
Trop cool: Too cool
Truc: Thing
Vachement: Very
Zapper: To forget/ignore
Beurk: Yuck
Bouge: Move
Casse-toi: Get lost
Chanmé: Amazing
Flingue: Gun
Gueule: Mouth
Kif-kif: Same
Marrant: Funny

Meuflette: Girlfriend
Naze: Lame
Osef: I don't care
Pétard: Joint
Poteau: Idiot
Quoi?: What?
Relou: Annoying
Sape: Outfit
Teuf: Party
Trop fort: Too good
Vénère: Angry
Zouz: Girl

Remember that slang terms are often used in informal or casual settings and may not be suitable for formal situations.

Conclusion

In conclusion, Biarritz is a captivating destination that offers a perfect blend of natural beauty, vibrant culture, and exciting activities. By following these comprehensive travel tips, you can make the most of your trip to Biarritz:

Choose the best time to visit, considering the weather and crowd preferences.

Plan your transportation and make necessary arrangements to reach Biarritz conveniently.

Find suitable accommodation options that cater to your preferences and budget.

Explore the top attractions, from breathtaking beaches to historical landmarks, and immerse yourself in the city's charm.

Engage in outdoor activities such as surfing, hiking, and golfing to make the most of Biarritz's stunning landscapes.

Delight in the rich Basque culture and cuisine, indulging in traditional dishes and discovering local traditions.

Experience the vibrant shopping scene and explore the bustling markets for unique souvenirs and local products.

Take advantage of Biarritz's strategic location and embark on day trips to nearby destinations to further expand your exploration.

Familiarize yourself with practical information, including local customs, emergency services, and any specific regulations or guidelines.

Check out the exciting events and festivals happening in Biarritz during your visit to immerse yourself in the local atmosphere.

Utilize various transportation options within Biarritz, such as walking, public buses, bicycles, taxis, and rental cars, to navigate the city conveniently.

Prioritize safety and health by adhering to general safety precautions, carrying travel insurance, and being aware of emergency services and medical facilities.

Embrace sustainable tourism practices to minimize your environmental impact and support the local community.

Learn a few basic French phrases and respect the local culture to enhance your interactions with the people of Biarritz.

By incorporating these travel tips into your itinerary, you can have a memorable and fulfilling experience in Biarritz, creating lasting memories of this remarkable destination. So, pack your bags, embrace the charm of Biarritz, and embark on an unforgettable adventure in this coastal gem of the Basque Country. Bon voyage!

Printed in Great Britain
by Amazon

25861042R00040